GW00602750

On Your
First Communion

Selected by

Peter Dainty

kevin
mayhew

Our Father in heaven,
   may your name be honoured,
   may your kingdom come,
   may your will be done
   here on earth,
   just as it is in heaven.
Give us the bread we need
   for today.
Forgive us the bad things
   that we have said or done,
   and help us to forgive
   those who have said and done
   bad things to us.
Help us to resist temptation,
   and keep us safe from evil.
For yours is the kingdom,
   the power and the glory,
   for ever and ever.
Amen.

Confession and forgiveness

O God, my loving Father,
    I am sorry for all my sins;
    I am sorry for not loving
    other people
    and for not loving you.
Help me to live in love
    as Jesus came to show me
    and give me your help
    not to sin again.
Amen.

Joan Brown

Loving Father God,
  I praise and thank you.
You are great
  and you are wonderful.
Thank you for sending Jesus
  to be my friend and to help me.
Thank you for sending
  your Holy Spirit
  to make me strong.
Thank you for
  forgiving my sins
  and for loving me for ever.

Joan Brown

Communion Prayers

Lord Jesus,
  thank you for inviting me
  to come to your table
  to eat your bread
  and to drink your wine,
  because then I know
  that I am one of your family,
  and it is a very special time for me.

Peter Dainty

Lord Jesus,
  I can't understand
  why you loved me so much
  that you gave your life for me,
  but as I receive
  your bread and wine
  I know that you are
  my closest Friend.

Peter Dainty

Heavenly Father,
   the bread is very small
   and we only get a sip of wine.
But we know that your love is very big
   for all the people in the world,
   because you gave your Son
   to die on a cross
   and show us
   how much you love us.

Peter Dainty

Holy Father,
    when I come to Communion
    I feel that I'm not good enough
    to receive the bread and wine.
But then I remember
    that Jesus gave
    his body and blood for me
    to make me better.
So as I eat and drink,
    please put your good Spirit in me.

Peter Dainty

9

Sometimes, Lord Jesus,
   people have to queue up
   for bread, because they're hungry
   but as we walk down the aisle
   and hold out our hands,
   it's as if we're queuing up for love,
   because that's what we're hungry for –
   something more than bread.
And we taste your love
   in the bread and wine,
   because they are signs
   of your broken body
   and your poured-out blood.
Love cost a lot to you,
   but to us you give it freely.
Thank you, Lord Jesus.
Amen.

Peter Dainty

Dear Jesus,
in the prayer you taught us
we ask for our daily bread
and we remember those
who don't have much to eat.
Is it because we haven't learnt
how to share our bread,
like we do
in Holy Communion?
Lord, make us as ready to give
as we are to receive.
Amen.

Peter Dainty

11

Blessed are you,
  Lord God of all creation.
Through your goodness
  we have this bread to share,
  fruit of the earth
  and the work of human hands.

Blessed are you,
  Lord God of all creation.
Through your goodness
  we have this wine to share,
  fruit of the earth
  and the work of human hands.

Joan Brown

Lord God, Almighty Father,
  it is right always and everywhere
  to give you thanks and praise:
  for the morning sun
  over mountains and seas,
  for the wind that blows
  and the river that flows,
  for the birds in the sky
  and the flowers of the field.
I praise and thank you,
  Lord my God, for my daily bread —
  for everything!

Joan Brown

Jesus,
   you died for me.
Your body is the broken bread
   I share in Holy Communion.
Your spilt blood
   is given in the wine.

But you defeated death,
   and no earthly rock
   could hold you down.

Because of you,
   I am raised up too.
Thank you
   for the gift of eternal life.
Amen.

Susan Hardwick

Lord Jesus,
　　I like the quietness
　　of Holy Communion —
　　quiet voices,
　　quiet feet,
　　quiet music.
We are quiet,
　　because we know
　　that you are here.
Your Spirit whispers to us.
Your holiness
　　is all around us,
　　as you feed us
　　with the bread and wine.
Was it like that
　　at the Last Supper?

Peter Dainty

It is a thing most wonderful,
  almost too wonderful to be,
  that God's own Son
  should come from heaven,
  and die to save a child like me.

And yet I know that it is true;
  he chose a poor and humble lot,
  and wept and toiled
  and mourned and died,
  for love of those who loved him not.

I sometimes think about the cross,
  and shut my eyes and try to see
  the cruel nails and crown of thorns,
  and Jesus crucified for me.

It is most wonderful to know
  his love for me so free and sure;
  but more amazing still to see
  my love for him so faint and poor.

And yet I want to love you, Lord;
  O light the flame within my heart.
  I will not rest until your love
  fills my life in every part.

William Walsham How (1823-97)

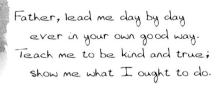

Father, lead me day by day
ever in your own good way.
Teach me to be kind and true;
show me what I ought to do.

When in danger make me brave;
make me know that you can save.
Keep me safely by your side;
let me in your love abide.

When I'm tempted to do wrong,
make me steadfast, wise and strong.
And when all alone I stand,
shield me with your mighty hand.

May I see the good and right
when they pass before my sight.
May I recognise your voice
when I hear the wise rejoice.

John Page Hopps (1834-1912)

Loving Jesus, good and kind,
    make me good and kind like you.
Hold my hand and make me strong;
    stay with me the whole day through.

Loving Jesus, true and wise,
    make me true and wise like you.
Fill my mind with loving thoughts;
    guide the things I say and do.

Loving Jesus, strong and brave,
    make me strong and brave like you:
strong to stand against all ill,
    brave to stand for all that's true.

Peter Dainty

Lord Jesus,
    thank you for
    a really good day out today.
We went to ...(say where)...
    and had a brilliant time.
We ...(say what you did)...
    and the best thing I liked was ...
    ...(say what it was)...
Thank you, Jesus,
    for a day to remember.
Amen.

Peter Dainty

Father in heaven,
   thank you for making the world.
Thank you for the sunshine
   in the summer,
   and the snow in the winter;
   for the flowers and birds in spring,
   and the coloured leaves
   on the trees in autumn.
Thank you for my family,
   and all my friends;
   for games to play,
   and places to visit,
   and things to learn;
   for pets and animals
   and books and computers,
   TV and videos and music,
   bikes and cars and aeroplanes...

There are so many good things
  to thank you for
  that I haven't time
  to say them all.
But thank you for Jesus,
  who came to show your love
  and teach us how
  to love one another
  and share
  all the good things
  in the world.
And thank you for our church
  where we can praise you
  and say, 'Thank you, God,
  for everything.'
Amen.

Peter Dainty

Jesus,
   I'm not very happy today.
Something very bad has happened...
    ...(say what it is)...
   and it's made me very sad.
Help me, Jesus,
   and make things right again.

But if they can't be right again,
   still help me to come through.
Make me brave and strong.
Show me how to make
   the best of what's happened.
Bring something good
   out of something bad.
You will know what to do,
   even if I don't.
I'm relying on you, Jesus.
I know you won't let me down.
Amen.

Peter Dainty

Lord Jesus,
   I'm sorry I let you down today.
I told a lie to get out of trouble,
   but it got somebody else
   in trouble instead.
Give me the courage to own up
   and say I'm sorry.
Then help me to face up
   to what they say and do.
They might forgive me
   or they might not.
I just don't know.
   But I don't like this nasty feeling
   I've got inside
   because I've let you down
   by not telling the truth.
   Help me to put things right, Lord,
Amen.

Peter Dainty

23

Heavenly Father,
   thank you for forgiving me.
It makes me feel
   so happy inside.
Everything seems alright again now;
   and I'd thought it never would.
I was so worried about
   owning up to what I'd done.
But they seemed to understand.
I couldn't believe it.

,So thank you for helping me.
I'll try not to do it again.
Amen.

Peter Dainty

Heavenly Father,
   I'm very worried about tomorrow,
   and frightened of
   what's going to happen...
   ...(say what it is)...
Give me strength,
   and help me through.
I can't face it
   without you.
Please be with me.
Amen.

Peter Dainty

Heavenly Father,
   thank you for helping me today.
I was so worried about it yesterday,
   but when it came,
   it wasn't as bad as I'd thought.
Thank you for being with me
   and helping me through.
Amen.

Peter Dainty

Dear God,
   I needed help today,
   because ...(say why)...
   and you sent someone to help me.
They just happened to be there
   when I needed them.
Thank you for knowing where I am
   and what I'm doing.
And thank you for sending someone
   to help me out.
May I be ready to help someone else
   whenever I can.
Amen.

Peter Dainty

Morning

Father, I thank you for today.
Help me to do my best
   in every task,
   and to make the most
   of every opportunity
   for doing good.
May I not give up difficult work
   too easily,
   but learn to achieve new things
   with patience and determination.
If I fail at anything
   may I be willing to try again,
   and get better each time.
May I not be moody or irritable,
   selfish or rude,
   disobedient or thoughtless.
But help me to treat other people
   as I would like them to treat me.
So may I come to the end of the day,
   tired, but happy.
Amen.

Peter Dainty

Evening

Father, hear my bedtime prayers.
For every good thing I've enjoyed today,
   thank you.
For every difficulty I have overcome,
   thank you.
For everything I've done well,
   thank you.
For help and kindness
   from other people,
   thank you.

For anything I've done wrong
   forgive me.
For being hurtful to other people,
   forgive me, and help me to be better
   tomorrow.

Now be with me while I sleep,
   so that I get up in the morning
   ready for anything –
   as long as you're by my side.
Amen.

Peter Dainty

Thank you, Lord Jesus,
   for all the good
   you have done for us
   by bearing so much pain for us.
Loving Saviour,
   Friend and Brother,
   help us to know you more clearly,
   love you more dearly
   and follow you more nearly,
   day by day.
Amen.

Based on a prayer by
St Richard of Chichester

First published in 2004 by

KEVIN MAYHEW LTD
Buxhall, Stowmarket, Suffolk, IP14 3BW
E-mail: info@kevinmayhewltd.com

9 8 7 6 5 4 3 2 1

ISBN 1 84417 347 X
Catalogue No. 1500759

Designed by Angela Selfe
Illustrations by Amanda Smith and Angela Palfrey

Printed and bound in China

First published in Great Britain in 1997 by
Brockhampton Press,
20 Bloomsbury Street,
London WC1B 3QA.
A member of the Hodder Headline Group.

This series of little gift books was made by Frances Banfield, Penny
Clarke, Clive Collins, Jack Cooper, Nick Diggory, John Dunne, David
Goodman, Paul Gregory, Douglas Hall, Lucinda Hawksley, Dicky
Howett, Dennis Hovell, Helen Johnson, C. M. Lee, John Maxwell,
Patrick McCreeth, Morse Modaberi, Sonya Newland, Anne Newman,
Terry Price, Mike Seabrook, Nigel Soper, Karen Sullivan, Nick Wells
and Matt Weyland.

ISBN 1 86019 561 X

A copy of the CIP data is available from the British Library upon
request.

Produced for Brockhampton Press by Flame Tree Publishing, a part
of The Foundry Creative Media Company Limited, The Long House,
Antrobus Road, Chiswick, London W4 5HY.

Printed and bound in Italy by L.E.G.O. Spa.

Just For You

IN SYMPATHY

Illustrated by

Douglas Hall
A.R.C.A.

Selected by Karen Sullivan

BROCKHAMPTON PRESS

In a gust of wind the white dew
On the Autumn grass
Scatters like a broken necklace.
Bunya No Asayasu, 'In a Gust of Wind'

Death always brings one suddenly face to face
with life. Nothing, not even the birth of one's
child, brings one so close to life as his death.
Frances Gunther, *Death Be Not Proud*

You're my friend,
So I brought you this book.
I give you this flower;
I hand you my hand.
John Marvin

Be assured when you see a tear on a cheek, a
heart is touched.

Anonymous

The strength of fire,
the taste of salmon,
the trail of the sun,
and the life that never goes away,
they speak to me.
And my heart soars.

Chief Dan George, 'My Heart Soars'

Death be not proud, though some have called thee
Mighty and dreadful, for thou art not so:
For those whom thou think'st thou dost overthrow
Die not, poor Death; not yet canst thou kill me.
From Rest and Sleep, which but thy picture be,
Much pleasure, then from thee much more must
flow;
And soonest our best men with thee do go —
Rest of their bones and souls' delivery!
Thou'rt slave to fate, chance, kings, and desperate
men,
And dost with poison, war and sickness dwell;
And poppy or charms can make us sleep as well
And better than they stroke. Why swell'st thou
then?
One short sleep past, we wake eternally,
And Death shall be no more: Death, thou shalt
die!

John Donne, 'Holy Sonnets'

It is not so much our friends' help that helps us as
the confidence of their help.

Epicurus

Thank Heaven! the crisis —
The danger, is past,
And the lingering illness,
Is over at last —
And the fever called 'Living'
Is conquered at last.

Edgar Allan Poe

Deep peace of the Running Wave to you.
Deep peace of the Flowing Air to you.
Deep peace of the Quiet Earth to you.
Deep peace of the Shining Stars to you.
Deep peace of the Son of Peace to you.

Celtic blessing

True friends have no solitary joy or sorrow.
William Ellery Channing

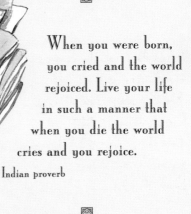

When you were born,
you cried and the world
rejoiced. Live your life
in such a manner that
when you die the world
cries and you rejoice.

Indian proverb

Death is the veil which those who live
call life:
They sleep, and it is lifted.
Percy Bysshe Shelley

When I am dead, my dearest,
  Sing no sad songs for me;
Plant thou no roses at my head,
  Nor shady cypress tree:
Be the green grass above me
  With showers and dewdrops wet;
And if thou wilt, remember,
  And if thou wilt, forget.

I shall not see the shadows,
  I shall not feel the rain;
I shall not hear the nightingale
  Sing on, as if in pain:
And dreaming through the twilight
  That doth not rise nor set,
Haply I may remember,
  And haply may forget.

Christina Rossetti, 'Song'

And I will show that nothing can happen
more beautiful than death.
Walt Whitman

In any man who dies there dies with him,
his first snow and kiss and fight . . . .
Not people die but worlds die in them.
Yevgeny Yevtushenko

If instead of a gem, or even a flower, we
should cast the gift of a loving thought
into the heart of a friend, that would be
giving as the angels give.
George Macdonald

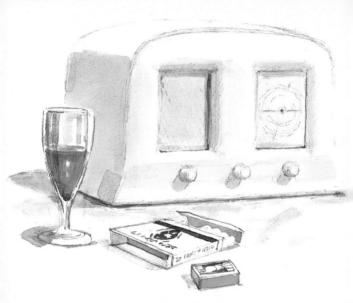

What you get is a living — what you give
is a life.
Lillian Gish

When sorrows come, they come not single spies,
But in battalions.
William Shakespeare, *Hamlet*

Sorrow makes us all children again, destroys all differences of intellect. The wisest knows nothing.
Ralph Waldo Emerson

What is life? It departs covertly. Like a thief Death took him.
John Gunther, *Death Be Not Proud*

The sorrow for the dead is the only sorrow from which we refuse to be divorced. Every other wound we seek to heal — every other affliction to forget: but this wound we consider it a duty to keep open — this affliction we cherish and brood over in solitude.
Washington Irving

Bereavement is a darkness
impenetrable to the
imagination of the
unbereaved.
Iris Murdoch

Weeping may endure for
a night, but joy cometh
in the morning.
Psalms, XXX:5

Human love and the delights of friendship, out
of which are built the memories that endure, are
also to be treasured up as hints of what shall be
hereafter.
Bede Jarrett

But what is all this fear of and opposition to
Oblivion? What is the matter with the soft
Darkness, the Dreamless Sleep?
James Thurber

※

The trumpet of a prophecy! O Wind,
If Winter comes, can Spring be far behind?
Percy Bysshe Shelley, 'Ode to the West Wind'

※

If, as I can't help suspecting, the dead also feel the
pains of separation (and this may be one of their
purgatorial sufferings), then for both lovers, and
for all pairs of lovers without exception,
bereavement is a universal and integral part of
our experience of love.
C. S. Lewis

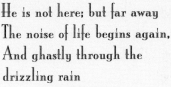

He is not here; but far away
The noise of life begins again,
And ghastly through the
drizzling rain
    On the bald street breaks
    the blank day.
Alfred, Lord Tennyson,
In Memoriam

Never does one feel one-
self so utterly helpless as
in trying to speak com-
fort for great bereave-
ment. I will not try it.
Time is the only comforter
for the loss of a mother.
Jane Welsh Carlyle

'Tis friends who make this desert world
To blossom as the rose;
Strew flowers o'er our rugged path,
Pour sunshine o'er our woes.
Anonymous

You will find as you look back upon your life
that the moments when you have really lived
are the moments when you have done
things in the spirit of love.
Henry Drummond

She was no longer wrestling with the grief, but
could sit down with it as a lasting companion and
make it a sharer in her thoughts.
George Eliot

Grief fills the room up of my absent child,
Lies in his bed, walks up and down with me,
Puts on his pretty looks, repeats his words.
William Shakespeare

The bitterest tears shed over graves are for words
left unsaid and deeds left undone.
Harriet Beecher Stowe

If I
Lie on my back and cry
Tears collect in my ears.
Eleanor Bron, 'Uncontrolled Experiment'

Widow. The word consumes itself . . . .
Sylvia Plath

Guilt is perhaps the most painful companion of
death.
Elisabeth Kübler-Ross

They wished and they murmured and whispered,
They said that to change was a crime.
Then a voice from nowhere answered,
'You must do what I say,' said Time.
Brian Patten, 'The Tree and the Pool'

No one ever told me that grief felt so like fear.
C. S. Lewis

If we could know
Which of us, darling, would be the first to go,
Who would be first to breast the swelling tide
And step alone upon the other side —
If we could know!

Julia Harris May

You will change,
Say the stars to the sun,
Says night to the stars.

Kathleen Raine, 'Change'

Peace, peace! he is not dead, he doth not sleep —
He hath awakened from the dream of life —
'Tis we, who lost in stormy visions, keep
With phantoms an unprofitable strife.

Percy Bysshe Shelley, *Adonais*

On a day of burial there is no perspective — for space itself is annihilated. Your dead friend is still a fragmentary being. The day you bury him is a day of chores and crowds, of hands false or true to be shaken, of the immediate cares of mourning. The dead friend will not really die until tomorrow, when silence is round you again. Then he will show himself complete, as he was — to tear himself away, as he was, from the substantial you. Only then will you cry out because of him who is leaving and whom you cannot detain.

Antoine de Saint-Exupéry

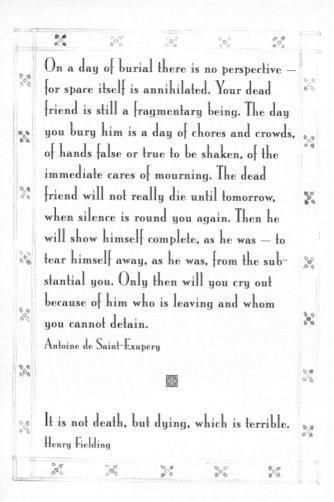

It is not death, but dying, which is terrible.

Henry Fielding

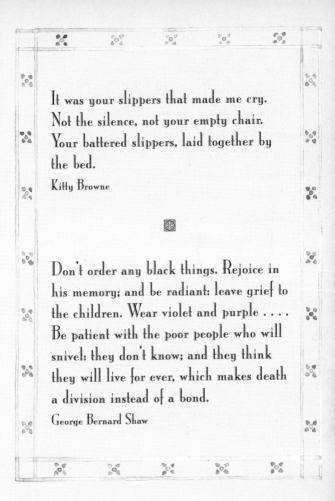

It was your slippers that made me cry.
Not the silence, not your empty chair.
Your battered slippers, laid together by
the bed.

Kitty Browne

Don't order any black things. Rejoice in
his memory; and be radiant: leave grief to
the children. Wear violet and purple . . . .
Be patient with the poor people who will
snivel: they don't know; and they think
they will live for ever, which makes death
a division instead of a bond.

George Bernard Shaw

God took her to Himself as you would lift a sleeping child from a dark, uneasy bed into your arms
and the light.

Robert Browning

What is heaven? 'tis a country
Far away from mortal ken;
'Tis a land, where, by God's bounty,
After death live righteous men.

That that blest land I may enter
Is my humble, earnest cry;
Lord! admit me to Thy presence,
Lord! admit me, or I die.

Christina Rossetti

The best remedy for those who are afraid, lonely or unhappy is to go outside, somewhere where they can be quiet, alone with the heavens, nature and God. Because only then does one feel that all is as it should be and that God wishes to see people happy, amidst the simple beauty of nature. As long as this exists, and it certainly always will, I know that then there will always be comfort for every sorrow, whatever the circumstances may be. And I firmly believe that nature brings solace in all troubles.

Anne Frank

Calm and deep peace on this high wold,
And on these dews that drench the furze,
And all the silvery gossamers
That twinkle into green and gold.
Alfred, Lord Tennyson, *In Memoriam*

But
Since he had
The genius to be loved, why let him have
The justice to be honoured in his grave.
Elizabeth Barrett Browning

Death will be the end of fear
and the fear of dying.
Ann Sexton, 'The Death King'

I have seen death too
often to believe in
death.
It is not an ending,
but a withdrawal.
As one who finishes
a long journey
Stills the motor,
turns off the lights,
Steps from his car,
And walks up the path
to the home that awaits
him.
Anonymous

Sun, shine bright on the blossoming trellises,
June and lavender, bring me hope.
John Betjeman, 'South London Sketch'

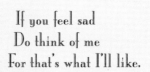

If you feel sad
Do think of me
For that's what I'll like.
When you live in
the heart
Of those you love
Remember then
You never die.

Rabindranath Tagore,
'Farewell my Friends'

Death stands above me, whispering low
I know not what into my ear:
Of his strange language all I know
Is, there is not a word of fear.

Walter Savage Landor

Sleep, oh sleep in the quiet of quietness,
Sleep, oh sleep in the way of guidance,
Sleep, oh sleep in the love of all loving.

Celtic blessing

Tread lightly, she is near
Under the snow,
Speak gently, she can hear
The daisies grow.

Peace, Peace, she cannot hear
Lyre or sonnet,
All my life's buried here,
Heap earth upon it.

Oscar Wilde, 'Rosa Mystica'

Does the road wind uphill all the way?
    Yes, to the very end.
Will the day's journey take the whole day long?
    From morn to night, my friend.

Christina Rossetti, 'Up-Hill'

Out of the dusk a shadow;
Then, a spark;
Out of the cloud a silence,
Then, a lark;
Out of the heart a rapture,
Then, a pain;
Out of the dead, cold ashes,
Life Again.

J. B. Tabb, 'Evolution'

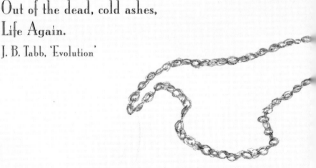

The Lord is my shepherd; I shall not want.
He maketh me to lie down in green pastures;
He leadeth me beside the still waters.
He restoreth my soul.

Psalms, XXIII

I do not believe that any man
fears to be dead, but only the
stroke of death.

Francis Bacon

No one's death comes to pass without making some impression, and
those close to the deceased inherit
part of the liberated soul and become richer in
their humaneness.

Hermann Broch

When one man dies, one
chapter is not torn out of
the book, but translated
into a better language.

John Donne

Death is the last enemy:
once we've got past that I
think everything will be alright.

Alice Thomas Ellis

For the sword outwears its sheath,
And the soul wears out the breast.
And the heart must pause to breathe,
And love itself have rest.

Lord Byron, 'So We'll Go No More A-Roving'

Sleeping at last, the struggle and horror past,
Sleeping at last, the trouble and tumult over,
Cold and white, out of sight of friend and lover,
Sleeping at last.

Christina Rossetti, 'Sleeping at Last'

The call of death is a call of love. Death can be sweet if we answer it in the affirmative, if we accept it as one of the great eternal forms of life and transformation.

Hermann Hesse

Death never takes
the wise man by
surprise,
He is always ready to go.

Jean de La Fontaine

Death cancels everything but truth; and strips a man of everything but genius and virtue. It is a sort of natural canonization. It makes the meanest of us sacred — it installs the poet in his immortality, and lifts him to the skies. Death is the greatest assayer of the sterling ore of talent. At his touch the drossy particles fall off — the irritable, the personal, the gross — and mingle with the dust; the finer and more ethereal part mounts with winged spirit to watch over our latest memory, and protect our bones from insult. We consign the least worthy qualities to oblivion, and cherish the nobler and imperishable nature with double pride and fondness.

William Hazlitt, on the death of Lord Byron

The loss of a beloved, deserving friend is the hardest trial of philosophy.

Lady Mary Wortley Montague

Because of its tremendous solemnity death is the light in which great passions, both good and bad, become transparent, no longer limited by outward appearances.

Søren Kierkegaard

Today when I see parents impatient or tired or bored with their children, I wish I could say to them, But they are alive, think of the wonder of that! They may be a care and a burden, but think, they are alive! You can touch them — what a miracle! You don't have to hold back sudden tears when you just see a headline about the Yale-Harvard game because you know your boy will never see the Yale-Harvard game, never see the house in Paris he was born in, never bring home his girl, and you will not hand down your jewels to his bride and will have no grandchildren to play with and spoil. Your sons and daughters are alive. Think of that — not dead but alive. Exult and sing.

Frances Gunther, *Death Be Not Proud*

How gladly would I meet,
Mortality, my sentence, and be earth
Insensible! How glad would lay me down,
As in my mother's lap! There I should rest,
And sleep secure.
John Milton

I don't think of all the misery, but of all the
beauty that still remains.
Anne Frank

Each day be joy to you,
No day be sad to you.
Honour and tenderness.
Celtic blessing

As death, when we come to consider it closely, is
the true goal of our existence, I have formed dur-
ing the last few years such close relations with
this best and truest friend of mankind, that his
image is not only no longer terrifying to me, but
is indeed very soothing and consoling! And I
thank my God for graciously granting me the
opportunity . . . of learning that death is the key
which unlocks the door to our true happiness.
Wolfgang Amadeus Mozart

45

The course of my long life hath reached at last
In fragile bark o'er a tempestuous sea
The common harbour, where must rendered be
Account for all the actions of the past.
Henry Wadsworth Longfellow

In the hour of misery, the eye turns to friendship.
In the hour of gladness, what is our want? It is
friendship.
Walter Savage Landor

I have known laughter — therefore I may sorrow
with you more tenderly . . . .
Garrison

The best portion of a good
man's life —
His little, nameless, unre-
membered acts
Of kindness and love.
William Wordsworth

When we lose a friend,
we die a little.
Louisa Booth

Those who love deeply
never grow old; they may
die of old age, but they die
young.
Sir Arthur Wing Pinero

Give your troubles to God; He will be
up all night anyway.

Anonymous

Men fear Death, as children fear to go
in the dark; and as that natural fear in
children is increased with tales, so is
the other.

Francis Bacon

For dust thou art, and unto dust thou
shalt return.

Genesis, III:19

Remember me when I am gone away,
  Gone far away into the silent land;
  When you can no more hold me by the hand,
Nor I half turn to go yet turning stay.
Remember me when no more day by day
  You tell me of our future that you planned:
  Only remember me; you understand
It will be late to counsel then or pray.
Yet if you should forget me for a while
  And afterwards remember, do not grieve:
  For if the darkness and corruption leave
  A vestige of the thoughts that once I had,
Better by far you should forget and smile
  Than that you should remember and be sad.

Christina Rossetti, 'Remember'

Even throughout life, 'tis
death that makes life life,
Gives it whatever the sig-
nificance.
Robert Browning

Death, in itself, is nothing; but
we fear
To be we know not what, we know not
where.
John Dryden

Death has a thousand doors to let out life: I shall
find one.
Philip Massinger

Do not go gentle into that good night,
Old age should burn and rave at close of day;
Rage, rage against the dying of the light.
Dylan Thomas, 'Do not go gentle into that good night'

I was there when you went —
I felt you go.
But then you were back, all around me
And you are there still
Wrapping me in the safety net of your memory.
Kitty Browne

Into each life some rain must fall.
Some days must be dark and dreary.

Henry Wadsworth Longfellow

I tell you, hopeless grief is passionless;
That only men incredulous of despair,
Half-taught in anguish, through the midnight air
Beat upward to God's throne in loud access
Of shrieking and reproach.
Elizabeth Barrett Browning

Sorrow is tranquillity remembered in emotion.
Dorothy Parker, 'Sentiment'

Build thee more stately mansions, O my soul,
As the swift seasons roll!
Leave thy low-vaulted past!
Oliver Wendell Holmes Sr, 'The Chambered Nautilus'

If I should die, think only this of me:
That there's some corner of a foreign field
That is forever England. There shall be
In that rich earth a richer dust concealed;
A dust whom England bore, shaped, made aware,
Gave, once, her flowers to love, her ways to roam,
A body of England's, breathing English air,
Washed by the rivers, blest by suns of home.

Rupert Brooke, 'The Soldier'

Life is real! Life is earnest!
And the grave is not its goal;
Dust thou art, to dust returnest,
Was not spoken of the soul.

Henry Wadsworth Longfellow

I see that I hold a sanctuary in their hearts, and in the hearts of their descendants, generations hence. I see her, an old woman, weeping for me on the anniversary of this day. I see her and her husband, their course done, lying side by side in their last earthly bed, and I know that each was not more honoured and held sacred in the other's soul, than I was in the souls of both.

Charles Dickens, *A Tale of Two Cities*

What does not recall her? I cannot look down to this floor, but her features are shaped on the flags! In every cloud, in every tree — filling the air at night, and caught by glimpses in every object by day, I am surrounded with her image! . . . . The entire world is a dreadful collection of memoranda that she did exist, and that I have lost her!

Emily Brontë, *Wuthering Heights*

They carried him very gently along the fields,
and down the lanes, and over the wide landscape;
Rachel always holding the hand in hers . . . .
The star had shown him where to find the God of
the poor, and through humility, and sorrow, and
forgiveness, he had gone to his Redeemer's rest.
Charles Dickens, *Hard Times*

Acknowledgements:

The Publishers wish to thank everyone who gave permission to reproduce the quotes in this book. Every effort has been made to contact the copyright holders, but in the event that an oversight has occurred, the publishers would be delighted to rectify any omissions in future editions of this book. Children's quotes printed courtesy of Herne Hill School; W. B. Yeats, from *The Lake Isle of Innisfree*, reprinted courtesy of A. P. Watt Ltd, on behalf of Anne and Michael Yeats, and taken from *The Collected Poems of W. B. Yeats*; *The Tree and the Pool*, by Brian Patten, reprinted courtesy of Viking Penguin, Kestrel; *Change*, by Kathleen Raine, reprinted courtesy of Golgonooza Press © Kathleen Raine; *The Death King*, by Anne Sexton, reprinted courtesy of Houghton Mifflin; John Betjeman © John Murray Publishers Limited and reprinted with their kind permission; Celtic Blessings translated by John and Caitlin Matthews, appearing in *The Little Book of Celtic Blessings* and *The Little Book of Celtic Wisdom* and reprinted courtesy of Element Books; Dorothy Parker quotes from *The Best of Dorothy Parker*, first published by Methuen in 1952, reprinted by Gerald Duckworth & Co., © Dorothy Parker, 1956, 1957, 1958, 1959, renewed; Sylvia Plath, *Widow*, in *Crossing the Water* (1971), reprinted courtesy of Faber & Faber Ltd; John and Frances Gunther in *Death be Not Proud* © John Gunther, reprinted courtesy of Harper & Row Publishers, Inc.

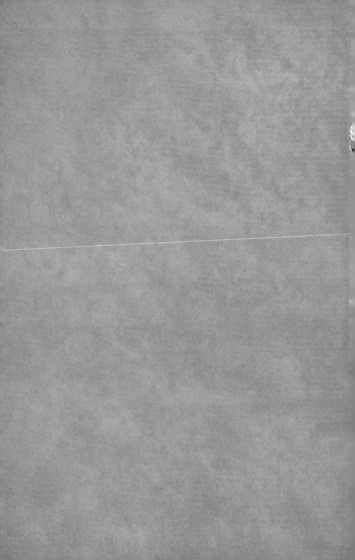